CHALLENGING LONELINESS
PATHS TO RECONNECT

ARTURO JOSÉ SÁNCHEZ HERNÁNDEZ

2024

CONTENTS

PREFACE

It's almost paradoxical that in an era when the world is so interconnected, and it's so easy to communicate with people on the other side of the planet, so many individuals still feel lonely. Often, this loneliness leads to such high levels of suffering that it significantly affects their quality of life. And while many believe this is an irremediable condition, the reality is that, in most cases, there are countless options to address it.

The main goal of this book is to invite readers to reflect on what they can do to prevent this state, and especially how to overcome it if they are already experiencing it.

While loneliness is also understood as the absence of company, which is often sought voluntarily and can even be necessary to work without distractions and organize one's thoughts, this work will only address the subjective perception of lacking certain emotional bonds or experiencing poor quality in them. In fact, if one chooses to live without certain emotional ties and still feels well, what is there to change in this regard?

This text starts a series of manuals dedicated to helping individuals face events that arise in the process of personal growth, such as loneliness, mistakes, frustrations, searching for a partner, jealousy, choosing friends, raising children, losing loved ones, romantic breakups, aging, and many more.

It consists of four chapters, general recommendations for overcoming the feeling of loneliness, and three glossaries. The first chapter defines what loneliness is and what it is not. The second explores its possible causes, the third examines ways of thinking, feeling, and acting that make it difficult or impossible to resolve, and the fourth offers strategies on how to organize oneself to overcome it and achieve a satisfying emotional life.

The general recommendations for overcoming the feeling of loneliness go through the main ideas presented in the study, which are offered by starting with a guideline or exhortation, explained concisely, and ending with a maxim, saying, or proverb.

Of the three glossaries, the first is dedicated to terms that allow for deeper insight into the issue of loneliness, the second to the negative moral qualities that hinder overcoming it, and the third to the positive qualities that make it possible to achieve a healthy emotional life. In all three cases, the terms are organized alphabetically.

Chapters three and four are subdivided into: Identifying the Problem, Mental Organization, Action, and Checking Results; offering the reader a more organized and thus more comfortable text to read.

The innovative aspect of this work lies in its structure, where, based on theoretical arguments, resources such as sayings, proverbs, images, and glossaries are integrated, complementing each other to increase the reader's understanding of the subject.

Sayings, proverbs, or maxims that are sometimes quite similar have been used, not out of fear of being misunderstood, as each group is preceded by an explanation, but rather so that readers can choose the one that best suits their lexicon and way of thinking.

This book is dedicated to anyone who feels lonely or wants to avoid feeling that way. It has been enriched from a practical perspective with interviews and focus groups involving people of both genders,[1] as well as with the author's experience in psychotherapy, where patients often mention feelings of loneliness.

The book compiles guiding and inspiring reflections, making it a suitable self-help material for readers, and a useful tool for those who practice psychotherapy.

Reality is always richer than any representation of it, and some specific cases may escape the logic of the arguments presented here. Nonetheless, if it helps improve the life of even a single person, the author would be more than satisfied.

Dr. Arturo José Sánchez Hernandez

The Author

~~~

Chapter I. WHAT LONELINESS IS AND WHAT IT IS NOT

In this section, we define what the feeling of loneliness is and what it should be differentiated from. We also describe the state of psychological disarray and collapse that it produces, which makes it difficult or impossible to overcome, along with some positive aspects of it.

"If you lack love, you are truly poor."

The feeling of loneliness could be defined as the perception of a lack or poor quality of emotional bonds, or of a particular bond that is felt to be very important.

– *"There is no greater poverty than not feeling loved."*

– *"Life, the emptier it is of love, the heavier it gets."*

It also involves feeling that you do not belong to any group with which you can share ideas, interests, and concerns.

– *"Feeling lonely is like being at a party where no one notices you."*

– *"A lonely person is like a plant without roots."*

11

It is experienced as a mix of anxiety, sadness, and great dissatisfaction and unhappiness.

    – *"Happiness and loneliness are incompatible."*

    – *"Loneliness is unbearable even in paradise." (Italy)[2]*

    – *"Wealth without company is not joy." (Spain)[3]*

"Loneliness is not being alone, it's feeling empty."

It is a subjective state that must be differentiated from the absence of company, which is often sought voluntarily and can even be necessary.

– *"Loneliness is not being able to be alone with yourself."*

– *"If you feel lonely when you're alone, you're in bad company."*

You can be without others, but if you feel loved and comfortable with yourself, there doesn't have to be any suffering.

– *"You won't feel lonely if you enjoy your own company when you're alone."*

"You can feel lonely while surrounded by people."

You can also be surrounded by people, even in a large crowd, and if you perceive the emptiness of lacking emotional bonds, suffering appears as an indicator of the discrepancy between current interpersonal relationships and the desired ones.

– *"The opposite of loneliness is not union or a crowd, but intimacy."*

– *"There is no worse loneliness than the one experienced while surrounded by people."*

"The eyes lunge, the feet tire, the hands cannot reach." (Spain)[4]

The distress of loneliness can lead to a state of psychological collapse and disarray in which nothing seems to go right, despite all the efforts made.

– *"To toil and toil, yet achieve little or nothing; this is many people's lament."*

"Banging your head won't break the wall."

Frustration increases psychological disarray and the inefficacy of actions.

– *"Desperation has never made good deals."*

– *"Desperation solves nothing."*

– *"If you lose your head in tough situations, you'll only make things worse."*

– *"He who loses his head, loses himself."* (Afro-Cuban saying)[5]

As well as the mental turmoil that makes it difficult or impossible to think clearly and reflect on mistakes.

– *"Muddy water does not make a mirror."* (Spain)[6]

"If you keep doing the same thing, everything repeats."

All of this forms a vicious circle, leading to more of the same: disarray and sinking further into emotional isolation.

– *"If you don't change, life will repeat it for you."*

– *"If you want a positive change in your life, stop doing the same things."*

"The prod gets the ox out of the mud." (Cuba)[7]

However, loneliness does have its positive side. The suffering it brings can lead to making necessary changes.

– *"The yoke won't move if there is no goad." (Puerto Rico)[8]*

– *"Hot iron bends easily; the same goes for people." (Spain)[9]*

"If you're doing well, you won't move." (Spain)[10]

Such modifications wouldn't happen from a place of comfort.

– *"The blacksmith who works with cold iron wastes his time." (Spain)[11]*

– *"Be grateful for the drop that overflowed the cup; it was the seed of change you needed."*

"Some storms come to clear your path."

It can even be seen as an opportunity to leave behind unfulfilling relationships or situations, thus improving one's life.

– *"Sometimes in the winds of change, we find our true direction."*

– *"Not all storms come to disrupt your life; some come to clear your path."*

The feeling of loneliness varies from one person to another, including aspects such as the type of emotional bond perceived as lacking or deteriorated, its intensity—ranging from mild discomfort to intense suffering—the duration, which may be short or prolonged over years, and its causes, which will be addressed in the next chapter.

FINAL CONSIDERATIONS

The feeling of loneliness is experienced as a mix of anxiety, sadness, and great dissatisfaction and unhappiness. This stems from a perception of a lack or poor quality of emotional bonds, or of a particular bond that feels very important, as well as from not belonging to any group with which to share ideas, interests, and concerns.

This state is not necessarily related to the presence or absence of company, as an individual can feel lonely even when surrounded by people if they perceive a lack or poor quality of their emotional relationships. Similarly, they may be alone, but if they feel loved and are comfortable with themselves, there doesn't need to be a feeling of loneliness.

The intense distress results in psychological collapse and disarray, leading to ineffective actions that do not resolve the issue, which in turn causes frustration, more distress, and further psychological disarray—continuing the cycle of ineffective actions. All this leads to more of the same: sinking deeper into emotional isolation.

The suffering that accompanies the feeling of loneliness can lead to making necessary changes that wouldn't happen from a place of comfort, which could be considered a positive aspect of it.

~~~

Chapter II. POSSIBLE CAUSES

In this section, we analyze the most common circumstances that lead to the deterioration or breakup of emotional relationships. Understanding these causes is essential for avoiding those that can be modified or working on those whose effects are still reversible.

"You never forget someone important in your life,
you just learn to live without them."

Among these causes are life events that lead to the loss of contact with family members, friends, or coworkers, such as the loss of loved ones.

– *"Those who passed through our life and left light will shine in us forever."*

"Out of sight, out of heart." (Czech Republic)[12]

Physical separation due to romantic breakups, retirement, moving, migration, or debilitating illnesses that confine one to the home or health facilities.

– *"Absence is the enemy of love; as far from the eyes as far from the heart." (Cuba)[13]*

– *"Out of sight and out of heart are almost the same thing." (Spain)[14]*

Entering and staying for long periods in institutions such as prisons, boarding schools, homes, or nursing homes, where you don't know anyone, and the emotional bonds you had in the place you came from are either lost or weakened.

– *"Absence erases love." (Cuba)[15]*

– *"The absent grow further away each day." (Japan)[16]*

"The fruit grows slowly." (India)[17]

Or, after spending several years in these institutions, leaving and finding that there are no quality emotional relationships outside because there has not been enough time to create them.

– *"Every good thing requires its time to come to fruition."*

– *"Each thing in its own time." (Spain)[18]*

– *"In this world, everything has its time; there is a moment for everything that happens." (Ecclesiastes 3:1)[19]*

"Smoke and a sour face drive people out of the
house." (San Salvador)[20]

Other causes are related, more than to life events, to personal
characteristics that make interactions unpleasant and push
others away.

– *"By offending and mistreating others, we end up alone."*

– *"Those who sow offenses reap loneliness."*

"With a shoe too tight, no one walks comfortably."
(Spain)[21]

Sometimes, being unpleasant is due to excessive demands on others and oneself.

– *"The man who demands perfection in every detail will end up without companions."*

– *"Water that is too pure cannot have fish, and a man who is too demanding cannot have companions."*

– *"If you look for friends without flaws, you'll end up without affection." (Mexico)[22]*

– *"He who wants a mule without a blemish should walk on foot." (Spain)[23]*

"There is no wretch who doesn't see himself as good." (Spain)[24]

Interestingly, these individuals generally do not see themselves as unpleasant, which makes resolving their loneliness more difficult.

- *"No one smells their own farts, nor do they see their children as ugly." (Cuba)[25]*
- *"Some are as charming as a lead pipe but think they're a sweet treat."*

Sometimes the interactions are acceptable, even pleasant, but others keep their distance because there is no respect for what belongs to others, and trust that has been given is repeatedly broken.

- *"A great vice of man is betraying those who trust in him." (Afro-Cuban saying)[26]*
- *"The traitor is detested."*
- *"You can fool some people sometimes, but not everyone all the time." (Afro-Cuban saying)[27]*

"With too much shame, you neither dine nor have lunch." (Spain)[28]

Personal characteristics can also lead to loneliness by making it difficult or impossible to connect emotionally with others, as is the case with shyness or any kind of unproductive and unjustified social inhibition.

– *"Timidity is of no use to a man in need." (Latin proverb)*[29]

– *"Let those who are overly shy expect bad years ahead."*

"You can't be caressed through a thick armor."

Due to an overgrowth of defenses or exaggerated sensitivity, as with excessive distrust, interpersonal relationships are avoided, making it impossible for others to approach you emotionally.

– *"Keeping your guard up all the time makes you a loner."*

– *"Sometimes you hurt more with the shield than with the spear."*

"He who builds a wall ends up a prisoner of the
wall he built."

Other conditions that cause an overgrowth of defenses include resentment and excessive pride, which can lead to the dissolution or deterioration of relationships, often over trivial matters.

– *"Many people are alone because they build walls instead of bridges."*

– *"If you cross everyone off, you'll end up alone."*

– *"If you quarrel with the springs, you'll end up dying of thirst." (Malaysia)[30]*

– *"Pride makes you lose those close to you."*

Emotional bonds can fade away due to neglect, which can happen when priorities are misplaced, and too much time is dedicated to certain activities, leaving none for family or friends.

– *"He who makes the secondary the main thing does wrong." (Spain)[31]*

- *"Don't let the speed at which you live your life distance you from what really matters."*
- *"Value what you have; you could lose diamonds while collecting stones."*

"He who went to Seville lost his chair." (Spain)[32]

This is evident when a partner is neglected, causing the relationship to deteriorate to the point that it may dissolve.

- *"If you abandon the nest, consider it lost." (Spain)*[33]

- *"He who doesn't take care of what he has is likely to lose it." (Afro-Cuban saying)*[34]

- *"If you have a shop, mind it; otherwise, sell it." (Afro-Cuban saying)*[35]

- *"Sow distance, and you will reap forgetfulness."*

- *"He who is often absent soon ceases to be missed."*

Or when one is peripheral or absent in raising children, and the bond is not formed with the quality it deserves.

- *"It's foolish to expect much when you sow little." (Spain)*[36]

- *"Sow little, reap little; it can't be otherwise." (Spain)*[37]

– *"What is left to the wind, the wind takes away." (San Salvador)*[38]

– *"The ship that isn't moored goes adrift." (Afro-Cuban saying)*[39]

And generally, it's only after the loss occurs that people start to appreciate the qualities of those with whom they have lost the emotional bond.

– *"No one knows the good they have until they lose it." (Afro-Cuban saying)*[40]

– *"Value what you have before life teaches you to value what you lost."*

– *"Value people while you have them, not after you lose them."*

"Some are like a bottomless container for
affection; no matter how much love they receive,
it's never enough."

The feeling of loneliness can also stem from an excessively high need for affection, making the person always feel they lack it, even when they are receiving it in the quality and quantity needed.

– *"Nothing satisfies the dissatisfied." (Cuba)*[41]

– *"The worst illness is to be satisfied with nothing." (Scandinavia)*[42]

– *"The discontented cannot be happy."*

– *"A person can feel lonely even when many people love them."*

"Marry poorly and rage—both come together."
(Spain)[43]

Due to an inadequate choice of partner, one might end up living with someone with whom they don't share common interests or the desired emotional bond.

– *"He who marries poorly always cries." (Spain)*[44]

– *"From a love that doesn't suit you, many evils and few blessings." (Spain)*[45]

– *"Nothing is heavier than an ill-managed marriage."*

– *"Better to walk alone than marry poorly."*

–"It's better to be alone than in bad company."

Often, several of these causes are mixed in one individual, complicating their situation. Such is the case of an addict who may be unpleasant in their treatment of others, pushing them away.

–"Those who suffer from addiction lack love."

–"Addictions bring loneliness."

"Gambling and drinking lead to losing your home."

Since addicts dedicate too much time and effort to their excessive passions, they also neglect their emotional bonds, which deteriorate or dissolve.

–"Addictions in the household are like worms in vegetables."

"If you indulge without reason, don't lament your fate."

With so many negative repercussions on interpersonal relationships, addictions can lead to a gradual disconnection from emotional ties, leading to a true social death.

– *"Addictions kill bit by bit."*

– *"The addict is his own enemy."*

Several causes of loneliness can also converge in an elderly adult whose interpersonal interactions have diminished significantly after retirement, who suffers from illnesses that cause some degree of disability, who has lost several loved ones, and who is extremely distrustful and difficult to deal with.

– *"Old age has no cure, and youth doesn't last." (Galicia)*[46]

– *"Illness and old age go hand in hand." (Spain)*[47]

Regardless of the causes of loneliness, individuals often adopt mental stances and behave in ways that, instead of solving the issue, only make it worse. This will be discussed in the next chapter.

FINAL CONSIDERATIONS

The causes of loneliness include:

Life events that cause sudden changes in emotional relationships, such as the loss of loved ones, romantic breakups, retirement, moving or migration, confinement to home or health facilities, entering institutions such as prisons, boarding schools, nursing homes, etc., or leaving them after several years and finding that there are no quality emotional relationships outside because there hasn't been enough time to create them.

Personal characteristics that gradually deteriorate emotional bonds, such as:

- Being unpleasant in interactions, which pushes others away.
- Unproductive social inhibitions that prevent or make it difficult for individuals to connect emotionally with others.
- Overgrown defenses, such as excessive distrust, which prevent others from connecting emotionally.

Neglecting certain emotional bonds, causing them to fade away or not develop.

Excessively high needs for affection, which makes individuals always feel they lack it, even when they are receiving it in the quality and quantity needed.

Poor partner selection, resulting in living with someone without shared interests or the desired emotional bond.

Being peripheral or absent in raising children, which prevents the development of filial love that one might later expect.

A combination of several causes, which complicates the situation further.

~~~

Chapter III. DYSFUNCTIONAL ATTITUDES

In this section, we analyze mental attitudes and behaviors that sabotage efforts to overcome the feeling of loneliness.

Identifying the Problem

"Some people are like the ostrich that buries its
head in the sand to avoid seeing things."

One such attitude is denying its existence, preventing the individual from recognizing or wanting to link their distress to the lack or poor quality of their emotional bonds.

– *"You can't cover the sun with a finger."*

– *"There is no worse blind person than the one who doesn't want to see, nor a worse deaf person than the one who doesn't want to hear." (Spain)*[48]

Not wanting to be aware of the problem that causes distress prevents addressing it and organizing oneself to solve it.

– *"The evil we do not know, we cannot eliminate." (Afro-Cuban saying)*[49]

– "No cure is possible for an unknown illness." (Latin proverb)[50]

– "Avoiding problems you need to face is avoiding the life you need to live."

"No matter how tightly we close our eyes, reality doesn't disappear." (Afro-Cuban saying)[51]

With this attitude of turning one's back on distress, the discomfort does not vanish.

– "Not wanting to see cannot stop time." (Afro-Cuban saying)[52]

– "You can deny reality, but that doesn't mean it will cease to exist."

Instead, it persists and, in many cases, worsens because denial prevents taking effective action.

– "You can evade reality, but not the consequences of evading it."

– "With closed eyes, you cannot move forward." (Afro-Cuban saying)[53]

– *"The one who keeps their eyes closed doesn't live in reality." (Afro-Cuban saying)*[54]

"Some people drown in a glass of water."

At the other extreme of denial is magnifying the problem and experiencing it as an unbearable misfortune, often related to low frustration tolerance.

– *"Don't make a mountain out of a molehill or a storm in a teacup."*

– *"Sometimes we suffer more from how we interpret problems than from their real significance."*

– *"Worry often casts a great shadow on something small."*

"Tears don't let you see the road." (India)[55]

From this intense distressing attitude, it becomes difficult to think clearly and focus on the best solutions.

- *"One who, in the face of misfortune, becomes dazed and only cries; increases their pain without freeing themselves from it." (Panchatantra: 2,180)*[56]

- *"Shouting will not put out the fire." (Czechoslovakia)*[57]

- *"Those who despair in misfortune only make it worse." (India)*[58]

- *"If you lose your head in tough situations, you'll only make things worse."*

- *"Despair solves nothing."*

- *"The more you worry, the greater your loss." (Persian saying)*[59]

Mental Organization

"Your mind will believe what you tell it. If you say
you can't, you won't."

In this phase, one may see loneliness as something beyond
remedy, leading to resignation.

– *"If you think you can't, you won't."*

– *"If you think you're defeated, you are, because you won't
put in the effort."*

"Before trying to find someone to blame, ask
yourself about your own responsibility in what's
happening."

Blaming others without considering one's own share of
responsibility.

- *"Some create their own storms and then feel sad when it
  rains."*

- *"How can you blame the wind for the mess if you were the
  one who left the window open?"*

Taking on a victim mentality and self-pity when, often, a
significant part of the responsibility lies with oneself.

- *"If you play the helpless one, the universe will only give
  you crumbs."*

- *"Don't act like a victim in circumstances you created
  yourself."*

- *"Keep playing the victim in your drama, and the universe
  will keep sending you villains."*

Seeing the resolution of the problem as entirely dependent
on others, who are supposedly the ones to provide the

affection in the quantity and quality desired or to solve all the distress.

- *"The responsibility for your life is yours; don't hand it over to others."*
- *"If you can't catch fish, don't blame the sea." (Greece)*[60]
- *"If your happiness depends entirely on others, you'll be in trouble."*

"Not everything that weighs on you is yours to carry."

Taking on responsibilities that are not yours, which generally makes you feel guilty and constitutes a burden that makes it difficult or impossible to move forward.

– *"Undeserved guilt is a hindrance."*

– *"Some people feel they must pay for dishes someone else broke."*

– *"Taking responsibility for what is truly yours gives you strength and allows you to grow; guilt, especially undeserved guilt, victimizes and diminishes you."*

Both evasion and self-blame act as distractions that prevent learning from mistakes and designing the life one wants to live.

– *"Decide to be the protagonist instead of the victim."*

– *"If you avoid your responsibilities or take on those that aren't yours, you won't thrive."*

– *"Take charge of your life; victims do not succeed."*

"Lack of planning leads to ruin."

Failing to organize and leaving everything to improvisation results in disarray in actions and unnecessary waste of time and resources.

– *"The one who works diligently but without a method throws away with one hand what they earn with the other."*

Action

"The lying wolf catches no prey, nor does the
sleeping man achieve victory." (Scandinavia)[61]

In this phase, inadequate mental attitudes such as passivity
and resignation may lead to doing nothing to solve the
problem, allowing the suffering to persist or worsen.

– *"God gives a worm to every bird, but He doesn't bring it
to the nest."*

– *"God gives the nuts, but doesn't crack them." (Germany)*[62]

"If you want to gather honey, don't kick over the beehive." (USA)[63]

Trying to attract others emotionally with impositions that end up pushing them away, resulting in greater social isolation.

– *"Bananas don't ripen by beating them." (India)[64]*

– *"A little bile makes much honey bitter." (Spain)[65]*

– *"If you don't like what you're receiving, take a good look at what you're giving."*

Due to an inability to tolerate pain, one may attempt to escape it through desperate decisions that, instead of resolving it, make it worse and later lead to regret.

– *"Sometimes the remedy is worse than the disease." (Spain)[66]*

– *"Some seek refuge in a beehive." (Malaysia)[67]*

Among these desperate decisions is getting into harmful relationships just to avoid feeling lonely.

– *"Nothing makes us more vulnerable than loneliness."*

- *"The lonely person offers their hand too quickly to whoever they find."*
- *"The one who searches in haste grabs just anything." (Afro-Cuban saying)*[68]
- *"He who cannot stand being alone accepts any company out of desperation."*
- *"Loneliness is a bad advisor." (Mexico)*[69]

Trying to alleviate the distress with alcohol or other substances, which leads to new problems without resolving the loneliness, often making it worse.

- *"Some, to clean the crust from their eyes, end up plucking them out."*
- *"Some drink poison to quench their thirst."*

Or being excessively generous at the expense of creating a situation that causes great unease.

- *"I will help those in need without reducing myself to need."*
- *"Help your neighbor lift their load, but do not consider yourself obliged to carry it for them."*

Checking Results

"He ridicules himself who constantly repeats the
same mistake."

In this final phase, one may persist in the same actions
despite their proven ineffectiveness.

- *"The man who has made a mistake and doesn't correct it
  commits another mistake." (Confucius)*[70]

- *"To err is human; to persist in the mistake is foolish."*

- *"He who stumbles twice on the same stone deserves to
  break his head." (Spain)*[71]

- *"Many sufferings await the stubborn." (Ecclesiasticus
  3:27)*[72]

Knowing the most common mistakes made when trying to
solve loneliness is important but not enough. An organized
set of actions is needed, which will be discussed in the next
chapter.

FINAL CONSIDERATIONS

Among the dysfunctional attitudes towards loneliness are:

Recognition of the Problem:

- **Denying it**, which makes it difficult to address and organize oneself.
- **Magnifying it** and perceiving it as an unbearable situation, which prevents clear thinking and hinders the search for the best solutions.

Mental Organization:

- **Seeing it as a hopeless situation** or as a state whose solution depends entirely on others, leading to inaction.
- **Blaming others**, often leading to a victim mindset and self-pity, distancing oneself from effective solutions.
- **Taking on undeserved guilt**, which becomes a heavy burden and prevents focusing on the aspects that need to be changed.

Action:

- Trying to **attract others emotionally with impositions**, which ends up pushing them away.
- Being **irrationally generous**, often leading others to take advantage of excessive kindness, resulting in situations that may lead to regret.
- **Getting into harmful relationships** that bring more discomfort.
- **Taking refuge in work or substance use** (such as alcohol or drugs) to relieve suffering, leading to addictions that further isolate from others.

Checking Results:

–**Persisting in the same methods** despite their proven ineffectiveness, which leads to more of the same and tends to make the situation chronic.

~~~

Chapter IV. HOW TO ORGANIZE YOURSELF TO OVERCOME LONELINESS

In this section, we suggest ways to organize behavior and actions that may help overcome the feeling of loneliness.

Identifying the Problem

"To solve your problems, become aware."

To resolve this state, one must start by being aware that the absence or poor quality of certain emotional bonds is the cause of the distress.

- *"Awareness is the first step to healing."*
- *"It's tough to know what you'd rather ignore, but it's worse to ignore what you should know."*

"A well-defined problem is almost solved."

And specify which bonds are missing or don't have the desired quality.

– *"Knowing a problem is already more than half of its solution." (José Martí)*[73]

– *"To solve a problem, you first need to identify it."*

This recognition involves determining if the feeling of loneliness is due to an exaggerated need for affection that can never be fully satisfied.

– *"People don't love you the way you want, but the way they can."*

– *"Don't expect everyone to love you; many people don't even love themselves."*

Mental Organization

The feeling of loneliness should not be seen as something to resign oneself to, but as a situation that can be perfectly resolved.

"Adversity comes with instructions in hand." (England)[74]

"He who seeks shall find." (Afro-Cuban saying)[75]

In fact, there are many people who need and would be willing to share affection with us, and we with them; it's just a matter of finding them with the right methods and with the resources available.

> "Ask and it will be given to you; seek and you will find; knock and the door will be opened to you." (Matthew 7:7)[76]

"A bird in the hand is worth more than a hundred flying." (Spain)[77]

We need to be realistic about the options we have.

– *"Wars are only won with feet on the ground." (Afro-Cuban saying)[78]*

– *"Tales do not fill the belly." (Galicia, Spain)[79]*

– *"He who lives on illusions dies of disillusion." (Afro-Cuban saying)[80]*

"When there are no dogs, one hunts with cats."

This allows us to focus on solving the problem with the resources at hand, rather than wasting time complaining about what is missing.

- *"Knowing how to live is making the best of what life gives us."*
- *"Do what you can, with what you have, where you are." (Theodore Roosevelt)*[81]
- *"Everyone chews with the teeth they have."*
- *"Everyone plays with their own cards." (Cuba)*[82]

It's also useful to overcome the past to avoid unproductive comparisons and to share as fulfilling a life as possible with others.

- *"If you don't let go of the past, with what hand will you grasp the future?"*
- *"Letting go of the past is giving the future a chance."*
- *"Heal your wounds and offer a clean body and heart to those who come."*

"Two who love each other must be alike."
(Mexico)[83]

It is very beneficial to determine the personal characteristics with which we have great compatibility and hope to find to some extent in people with whom we wish to form emotional bonds, as well as the flaws that are highly incompatible to avoid future discomfort or breakups that could lead back to loneliness.

– *"Each one with their own match." (Spain)*[84]

– *"Every sheep with its partner." (Spain)*[85]

"No sky without clouds, no paradise without serpents."

However, be careful that these criteria are not so high that no one can meet them.

– *"He who wants a mule without flaws should walk on foot." (Spain)*[86]

– *"He who seeks a wife without flaws will remain unmarried." (Romania)*[87]

– *"There is no woman or mule without a single flaw."*

– *"Every mule limps on one leg." (Cuba)*[88]

– *"No rose without thorns." (Spain)*[89]

– *"No forest without dry branches." (Romania)*[90]

"To arrive, get organized."

Something of vital importance is establishing a plan to organize actions.

- *"Well-considered plans yield good results; those made hastily lead to ruin." (Proverbs 21:5)*[91]
- *"Action fulfills, but thought organizes action." (Afro-Cuban saying)*[92]
- *"When the right path is chosen, the goal is reached." (Afro-Cuban saying)*[93]
- *"Wars are won with good strategy." (Afro-Cuban saying)*[94]

Action

Then move on to action, as loneliness is a state that requires effort to overcome.

- *"Fortune favors those who seek it." (Spain)*[95]

"Without work, there are no cakes." (Czech Republic)[96]

59

"If you are friends with yourself, you will not feel alone."

It is helpful to incorporate activities and goals that make you feel useful and good about yourself, even in the absence of others, which boosts self-esteem and helps break the vicious cycle between deep psychological distress and the ineffectiveness of attempts to overcome it.

– *"Learn to be your own company."*

– *"Those who are accompanied by noble thoughts are never alone."*

Feeling good about oneself also prevents getting into unhealthy relationships or making decisions that may lead to foreseeable regret.

– *"Learn to be happy alone, so that companionship is a matter of choice, not necessity."*

– *"When you learn to love your own company, you'll be more careful in choosing with whom you spend your time."*

– *"Look for a partner when you're ready, not when you're lonely."*

"Familiarity breeds affection."

Proximity and repetition are key to forming emotional bonds, so it is helpful to place yourself in situations that increase the likelihood of contact and seeing the same faces repeatedly.

– *"From looking comes loving; from not seeing, comes forgetting."*

– *"Let them get used to your presence, and you to theirs."*

"You won't find fish in the treetops."

It is very helpful to visit places frequented by people with common interests and desired characteristics.

– *"Are you looking for fish? Don't climb a tree." (China)*[97]
– *"To fish for fish, go to the river." (Spain)*[98]

"Everything in its own time." (Czech Republic)[99]

Keep in mind that, even under the best conditions, every emotional bond has its own pace to form and strengthen.

– *"The orange ripens in its own time." (Cuba)[100]*

– *"Do you see a tree? Do you see how long it takes to hang the golden orange or the red pomegranate from the thick branch? By delving into life, you see that everything follows the same process. Love, like a tree, must go from seed to sapling, to flower, and to fruit." (José Martí)[101]*

"If you want to be loved, love and be kind."

Generally, we evoke reactions and feelings in others that are in line with how we treat them, so to awaken love in others towards us, we must be kind.

– *"Treatment is a psychic boomerang."*

– *"There is no sword against kindness." (Japan)*[102]

– *"He who satisfies will be satisfied."*[103]

This doesn't guarantee receiving the same in return, but it is an essential condition.

– *"Planting a seed is not enough for a plant to grow, but without a seed, there will be no plant."*

"Weapons, women, and books must be tended to every day." (Netherlands)[104]

This applies not only to forming new bonds but also to ensuring that existing ones don't fade away due to neglect.

– *"Orchards, mills, and women need continuous care."*

– *"If you have a shop, mind it." (Cuba)[105]*

"Fish or cut bait." (USA)[106]

If loneliness stems from the perception of a deteriorating romantic bond, it is necessary to evaluate it and either save it or let it go as circumstances require. Staying in a state of indecision only perpetuates the suffering.

– *"Either sing or be silent." (Spain)[107]*

– *"Take it or leave it." (Spain)[108]*

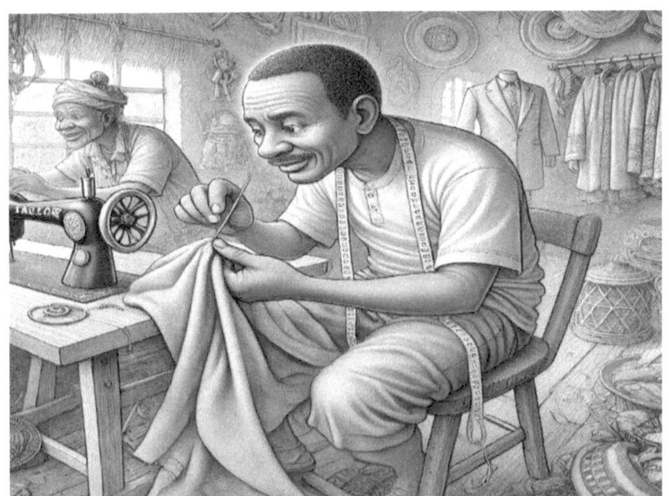

"A stitch in time saves nine."

Being timely and decisive allows you to tackle and solve the problem before it becomes more complicated.

– *"Prevent disorder before it gets bigger." (Lao Tzu)*[109]

– *"Fight the difficulty while it's easy; fight the big while it's small." (Lao Tzu)*[110]

Checking Results

"With one egg, you will not break the rock."
(Czechoslovakia)[111]

And finally, change if the means used are insufficient.

– *"You can't catch a hippo with a cast net." (Afro-Cuban saying)*[112]

– *"A gourd with a hole is no good for a drinking cup." (Cuba)*[113]

– *"A chair without a bottom is useless for sitting." (Afro-Cuban saying)*[114]

– *"A lamp without a wick—what use is it?" (Spain)*[115]

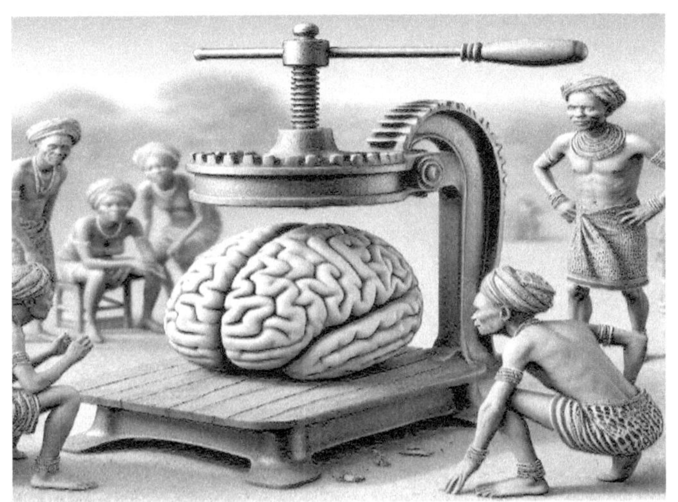

"Don't be rigid; pay attention to the results."

If the methods aren't being effective

- *"A shout won't kill a rabbit, even if it's well-aimed."*
- *"Running alone doesn't catch the birds." (Romania)*[116]
- *"If it doesn't work forwards, do it backwards." (Afro-Cuban saying)*[117]
- *"Don't fear necessary changes."*

"When the land doesn't yield, prepare to move."

Or if projects demand a price you're not willing to pay.

– *"A wise farmer doesn't till land that bears no fruit." (Spain)*[118]

– *"A business that doesn't profit should be left."*

– *"Don't look where there is nothing." (Spain)*[119]

– *"If something isn't progressing, let it go and move on."*

FINAL CONSIDERATIONS

To overcome loneliness, it is necessary to recognize it, organize mentally, and take action.

Recognize It:

- Define when loneliness is the cause of psychological distress.
- Identify the emotional bonds that are missing or lack the desired quality.

Mental Organization Includes:

- Determine if the feeling of lack is due to an exaggerated need for affection that can never be satisfied, and adjust expectations accordingly.
- See loneliness as a situation that can be perfectly resolved, which requires organizing oneself, adopting healthy mental attitudes, and acting in a timely manner.
- Be realistic about the options available, which allows focusing on solving the problem with the resources at hand, instead of wasting time complaining about what is missing.
- Overcome the past when the perception of lack is romantic in nature, which helps avoid unproductive comparisons and enables sharing a fulfilling life with new relationships that arise.
- Define personal characteristics that have high compatibility and that are desired in future emotional bonds, as well as the flaws that are highly incompatible to avoid future discomfort or breakups that could lead back to loneliness.
- Establish a strategy tailored to the particularities of the situation being experienced.

Take Action:

- Incorporate activities and goals that make you feel useful and good about yourself, even in the absence of others, which helps break the vicious cycle between psychological distress and the ineffectiveness of attempts to overcome it.
- Visit places frequented by people with common interests and desired characteristics, which increases the chances of contact and communication essential for forming emotional bonds.
- Give love, which is no guarantee of awakening loving feelings in others but is an essential condition.

Check Results Involves:

- Change if the means are insufficient, the methods are not effective, or the projects are demanding a price you are not willing to pay.

~~~

GENERAL RECOMMENDATIONS TO OVERCOME LONELINESS

In this section, we summarize the main ideas presented in this work, beginning with guidance or exhortation, explained concisely, and concluding with a maxim, proverb, or saying.

1-Recognize when your suffering is due to feelings of loneliness. Only by being aware of the cause of distress can you start to solve it. *-"To solve your problems, become aware."*

2-Identify the emotional bonds you feel are missing or lack the desired quality. This is precisely the key to loneliness as a problem to be solved, so understanding it is of vital importance. *-"Identifying a problem is a crucial part of its solution."*

3-Eliminate the causes of loneliness. By eliminating sources that are still modifiable, the situation often improves significantly or, at least, the same mistakes can be avoided. *-"The man who has made a mistake and doesn't correct it commits another mistake."* (Confucius)[120]

4-Adjust your expectations regarding the affection others can give you. Determine if the feeling of lack is due to an exaggerated need for affection that can never be satisfied. *-"People don't love you the way you want, but the way they can."*

5-See loneliness as a state that can be perfectly resolved. Generally, there are many people for each individual who need and would be willing to exchange affection with them. It's just a matter of finding them with the right methods and available resources. *-"Ask and it will be given to you; seek and you will find; knock and the door will be opened to you."*

6-Be diligent. Overcoming loneliness is usually not something that happens spontaneously. An active mental attitude is needed to carry out the corresponding actions. Passivity only maintains or worsens it. -*"God gives a worm to every bird, but He doesn't bring it to the nest."*

7-Don't make rash decisions just to escape distress. Don't let suffering lead you to desperate actions that you might regret later. -*"Don't make permanent decisions based on temporary emotions."*

8-Incorporate activities and goals that make you feel useful and good about yourself, even in the absence of others. We generally inspire in others feelings toward us similar to those we have for ourselves. Therefore, start by feeling good in the absence of others if you intend to overcome loneliness. -*"If you don't feel good about yourself, how can you make others feel comfortable in your presence?"*

9-Be realistic. Being objective about the real options available allows you to focus on solving the problem with the resources at hand, rather than wasting time complaining about what's missing. -*"Knowing how to live is making the best of what life gives us."*

10-When dealing with a deteriorating romantic bond: define it. If loneliness stems from a deteriorating romantic relationship, it is advisable to review it, then either save it or let it go, depending on the situation, but not remain in a state of indecision that perpetuates the suffering. -*"Fish or cut bait."* (United States of America)[121]

11-Overcome the past. Living anchored to the past prevents moving forward towards a future of new emotional bonds, so you must overcome it if you intend to share a fulfilling life with others. -*"It's difficult to build a future with someone who hasn't overcome their past."*

12-Establish a plan. Not everything can be left to improvisation. If you want to increase the chances of solving the problem, you must plan. *-"To arrive: get organized."*

13-Define the type of person you're interested in. Determine the personal characteristics with which you have great compatibility and those that cause great discomfort. This is a good step to avoid past mistakes and begin relationships with a minimum level of quality. *-"Each one with their own match."* (Spain)[122]

14-Focus on people who are emotionally attractive to you and don't torment yourself over those who aren't. To attract people emotionally, they must be susceptible to being attracted to us; otherwise, we waste time, resources, and become even more frustrated, increasing the feeling of loneliness. *-"A wise farmer doesn't till land that bears no fruit."*

15-Identify and develop your own interests. To share interests with others, you must first know and develop your own, as this increases the chances of connecting with people who share them and are similar to you in that sense. *-"Two who love each other must be alike."* (Mexico)[123]

16-Visit places frequented by people with common interests and desired characteristics. Putting yourself in the right place increases the chances of interacting with the right people to establish bonds that help overcome loneliness. *-"To fish for fish, go to the river."*

17-Proximity and repetition are key. To increase the chances of starting and deepening emotional bonds, it's also necessary to increase the chances of repeated contact and communication. Therefore, it's advisable to put yourself in situations where you see the same faces over and over. *-"Familiarity breeds affection."*

18-If you want to be loved, love and be kind. People are attracted emotionally through love, services, and kindness, not through demands and harshness.-*"If you don't like what you're receiving, take a good look at what you're giving."*

19-Love and respect yourself if you want others to do so. For others to love and respect us, it's essential to love and respect ourselves. Trying to form or maintain an emotional bond at any cost generally leads to disdain and abusive actions toward us. -*"Love enters through respect; you can't love someone you despise."* (José Martí)[124]

20-Respect the pace and timing of each emotional relationship. You can't aspire to instant intimacy. Each emotional bond requires time to form and consolidate, so it's necessary to know how to wait. -*"The orange ripens in its own time."* (Cuba)[125]

21-After forming emotional bonds, be attentive and detail-oriented. It's important that the initiatives that led to a stable relationship you want to maintain continue, at least to some extent, to prevent it from fading due to neglect. -*"If you have a shop, mind it."* (Cuba)[126]

22-If what you're doing isn't working, change. If you still feel you're not progressing, even with techniques that might be considered appropriate, don't hesitate to change methods, procedures, or even projects. -*"If something isn't progressing, let it go and move forward yourself."*

~~~

GLOSSARIES

En esta sección encontrarás tres glosarios. El primero está dedicado a términos que nos ayudan a entender los desafíos de la soledad, el segundo se enfoca en las cualidades morales negativas que dificultan superarla, y el tercero explora las cualidades positivas que pueden conducir a una vida emocional plena.

THEORY OF LONELINESS

Acceptance-Belonging Needs: The need to belong, be accepted, and occupy a valued position within a social group.

Affection Seeker: Someone with an excessive need for affection who tends to feel frustrated when the amount they receive from others seems inadequate to them.

Attachment (Basic Functions): Ensures protection for survival and provides a sense of security.

Attachment (Complementary Functions): Helps regulate stimulation, promotes exploration and learning, supports physical and mental health, fosters social development, and provides emotional satisfaction.

Attachment: An intense and lasting emotional bond formed through reciprocal interactions, aimed at providing safety, comfort, and proximity during times of need or threat.

Change Fallacy: The mistaken belief that one's well-being is entirely dependent on the actions of others.

Companion Loneliness (Emotional Isolation in Company): The experience of feeling emotionally disconnected or isolated even when surrounded by people and having a social support network, yet lacking emotional fulfillment.

Detachment: A state in which a person distances themselves emotionally from people, objects, or circumstances, achieving a greater sense of independence.

Diogenes Syndrome: A behavioral disorder, often affecting older adults, marked by self-neglect, voluntary isolation, and the accumulation of trash and waste in the home.

Family Helplessness: The lack of protection, defense, or support from one's family, leading to a sense of vulnerability.

Family Support: The protection, defense, and assistance provided by a family to one of its members.

Frustration (Intolerance to): An exaggerated sensitivity to setbacks or delays in fulfilling desires, often resulting in impulsive actions to either gain immediate pleasure or avoid discomfort.

Frustration: An emotional response characterized by anger and disappointment when one perceives obstacles to achieving personal goals, with the intensity growing as obstacles or desires increase.

Happiness: A temporary state of well-being and satisfaction that occurs when one achieves goals that align with a meaningful purpose, often including aspects of social contribution and service to others.

Helplessness: The absence of protection, defense, or support, leaving someone vulnerable.

Hermit: A person who chooses to live in seclusion, often leading a solitary and ascetic life away from social ties.

Intimacy: A personal emotional space characterized by deep aspects of an individual's emotional life, or close, trusting relationships where participants share deeply personal emotions.

Involuntary Social Isolation: A condition where a person or group lacks social relationships or interactions for reasons beyond their control, such as imprisonment, exile, migration, or the loss of loved ones.

Loneliness (Classification): Different ways to categorize loneliness, including: 1- The intensity of discomfort: mild, moderate, severe. 2- The perceived lack of a specific type of bond: family, romantic, friendship. 3- Duration: short-term or long-term. 4- Causes: loss of loved ones, romantic breakups, migration, or personal traits that hinder forming bonds.

Loneliness (Feeling of): A subjective state where one perceives a lack of meaningful emotional bonds or lacks a group with which to share ideas and interests. It is often experienced as a mix of anxiety, sadness, dissatisfaction, and unhappiness. (See involuntary and voluntary social isolation)

Loneliness (Levels): The varying intensity of discomfort from loneliness, ranging from mild unease to severe emotional suffering.

Loneliness: The state of being without emotional or physical companionship, leading to feelings of disconnection.

Privacy: A personal aspect of someone's life that is meant to be kept private and confidential, away from public scrutiny.

Rejection or Social Exclusion: A deliberate and punitive act of separating an individual or group from certain social relationships or interactions, such as through imprisonment.

Relationship-Connection Needs: The need for connection and bonding with others to experience a fulfilling life and form a sense of identity.

Social Death: The loss of meaningful social ties, leaving an individual isolated and potentially involved in self-destructive activities, such as substance abuse.

Social Support Network: A group of people or communities one can rely on for support, whether for meeting needs or solving personal challenges.

Support: Protection, defense, or assistance that one person or entity offers to another to ensure safety and well-being.

Voluntary Social Isolation: A condition where a person or group deliberately decides to be without certain social relationships or interactions, such as during a spiritual retreat, when a scientist isolates themselves to complete a project, or when someone decides to live without a stable partner.

~~~

NEGATIVE MORAL QUALITIES

Annoyance: A quality of being bothersome, unpleasant, or overly intrusive in interactions with others.

Arrogance: The attitude of believing oneself to be excessively superior while looking down on others.

Belligerence: A tendency to engage in arguments or conflicts, often with a confrontational attitude.

Brutality: A propensity for violent and excessive behavior, often without regard for others.

Dependence: A state where an individual cannot take care of themselves or act independently.

Depravity: The condition of being morally corrupt or engaging in degenerate behavior.

Disloyalty: The quality of failing to demonstrate loyalty, betraying trust or commitment.

Dissatisfaction: The state of not being content or happy with what one receives or experiences.

Egocentrism: An exaggerated focus on oneself, often considering oneself the center of attention and activity.

Escapism: The inclination to avoid facing problems or conflicts by withdrawing or seeking distractions.

Evasiveness: A tendency to avoid responsibilities, decisions, or challenges that require attention.
~~~

Harshness: A lack of kindness or gentleness in dealing with others, resulting in a tough or unfriendly demeanor.

Hostility: A feeling of animosity or strong dislike towards one or more people, often leading to conflict.

Immaturity: A lack of sufficient development in one's abilities to fulfill social roles and responsibilities.

Impulsiveness: The lack of forethought or planning before acting, often resulting in unconsidered behavior.

Indelicacy: A lack of sensitivity or courtesy in dealing with others, often causing discomfort or offense.

Inflexibility: An inability or unwillingness to change one's thoughts, feelings, or behaviors when needed.

Intolerance: A lack of respect or acceptance for ideas, beliefs, or practices that are different from one's own.

Malice: A tendency to think or act with harmful intentions, often with ill will towards others.

Misanthropy: A dislike or hatred towards other human beings, leading to social withdrawal.

Misogyny: A dislike or hatred directed specifically at women or girls, often leading to discriminatory behavior.

Opportunism: A tendency to seek advantages in situations or dealings, often without regard for fairness.

Passivity: The unwillingness to take action when faced with situations requiring intervention or help.

Resentment: Deep-rooted bitterness or lingering anger towards someone due to a perceived wrong.

Rudeness: A lack of politeness expressed through discourteous or disrespectful words or actions.

Self-Contempt: A feeling of disdain towards oneself, typically linked to low self-esteem.

Selfishness: An attitude where one's own interests are prioritized over all other considerations.

Self-Pity: The feeling of sympathy and sorrow for oneself, often focusing on personal suffering.

Sensitivity: Overreacting to minor issues, often taking offense easily and becoming upset by trivial matters.

Stubbornness: Persistent refusal to change a mistaken belief or behavior, even when proven wrong.

Submission: A state where one's judgment, decisions, or feelings are entirely subordinated to another person's.

Timidity: A behavior marked by social inhibition, often due to unfounded fears or lack of confidence.

Unapproachability: The quality of being unsociable or having a rough temperament, making it hard for others to engage.

Untimeliness: Actions or words that are out of place, lacking consideration for the right time or context.

Vilification: The quality of being untrustworthy or dishonorable, betraying the trust placed in them.

Whining: A habit of frequently complaining, often without substantial cause or reason.

Withdrawal: A tendency to be reserved, avoiding communication and social interaction with others.

~~~

POSITIVE MORAL QUALITIES

Affability: The quality of being pleasant, gentle, and kind in conversation and interactions with others.

Affection: The quality of being loving and caring towards others, expressing warmth and tenderness.

Assertiveness: The ability to stand up for one's rights while respecting the rights of others.

Charity: The habit of doing good and providing help to those in need without expecting anything in return.
~~~

Courtesy: The set of actions and expressions used to show attention, consideration, politeness, and respect in social interactions.

Flexibility: The ability to adapt one's activities and behaviors to achieve objectives, based on changes in both the external environment and oneself.

Foresight: The quality of making preparations to handle foreseeable contingencies or needs effectively.

Generosity: The quality of being inclined to give gifts or offer services willingly and with a sense of grace and timing.

Kindness: The quality of behaving in a way that makes one deserving of love, through actions and treatment of others.

Objectivity: The quality of analyzing situations dispassionately, focusing on reality and facts rather than emotions.

Opportunity: The skill of recognizing favorable circumstances for action or speech, and making the best use of them.

Philanthropy: Love for humankind expressed through selfless assistance and support for others.

Politeness: The quality of being considerate, attentive, and treating others with good manners and respect.

Providence: Taking measures to achieve a goal, as well as making arrangements to minimize the consequences of an adverse event.

Responsibility: The quality of paying due attention to problems and decisions, accepting the consequences of one's actions.

Sociability: The natural inclination to interact with and relate to other people, enjoying their company.

Solidarity: Mutual support and assistance among members of a group, fostering unity.

Sympathy: A way of being that makes a person appealing or pleasant to others, fostering a sense of connection.

Tact: The prudence and sensitivity needed to handle delicate situations with care.

Tolerance: Respect, understanding, and acceptance of others' ideas, beliefs, or practices as their rightful choices.

~~~

BIBLIOGRAPHIC REFERENCES AND NOTES

1- Topics discussed: 1- Causes of loneliness, 2- Dysfunctional mental attitudes or postures that hinder or prevent overcoming loneliness, 3- Functional ways to organize oneself to overcome loneliness. The questions were: 1- What do you consider could be the causes of people feeling lonely? 2- What do you think people do wrong when they feel lonely that prevents them from getting out of that state? 3- How do you think people should organize themselves to overcome loneliness?

2- Feijóo, Samuel. The Wisdom of Juan Without Anything. Signs in the Expression of the People. Proverb. Santa Clara, Cuba: Revista Signos. No. 14. Year 5, No. 2; January-April 1974. p. 151.

3- Solís, José Antonio. Proverbs, Sayings, Idioms, and Sentences. All the Popular Wisdom of the People of Spain at Your Reach. Spain: El Arca de Papel Editores; 2003. p. 139.

4- Sintes Pros, Jorge. Dictionary of Aphorisms, Proverbs, and Sayings. Barcelona, Spain: Editorial Sintes; 1954. p. 103.

5- Valdés Jane, Ernesto. Divinatory Proverbs of the Caracol and Odun of Ifá. -In Cuban Santería- Documents for the History and Culture of Osha-Ifá in Cuba. Proverbs of (1-6) Okana tonti Obara. First Edition: Proyecto Orunmila; 2007. p. 2.

6- Feijóo, Samuel. The Wisdom of Juan Without Anything. Signs in the Expression of the People. Proverb. Santa Clara, Cuba: Revista Signos. No. 14. Year 5, No. 2; January-April 1974. p. 51.

7- Feijóo, Samuel. The Wisdom of Juan Without Anything. Signs in the Expression of the People. Proverb. Santa Clara, Cuba: Revista Signos. No. 14. Year 5, No. 2; January-April 1974. p. 83.

8- Feijóo, Samuel. *The Wisdom of Juan Without Anything. Signs in the Expression of the People. Proverb.* Santa Clara, Cuba: Revista Signos. No. 14. Year 5, No. 2; January-April 1974. p. 93.

9- Solís, José Antonio. *Proverbs, Sayings, Idioms, and Sentences. All the Popular Wisdom.* Spain: El Arca de Papel Editores; 2003. p. 75.

10- Solís, José Antonio. *Proverbs, Sayings, Idioms, and Sentences. All the Popular Wisdom of the People of Spain at Your Reach.* Spain: El Arca de Papel Editores; 2003. p. 142.

11- Solís, José Antonio. *Proverbs, Sayings, Idioms, and Sentences. All the Popular Wisdom.* Spain: El Arca de Papel Editores; 2003. p. 53.

12- Feijóo, Samuel. *The Wisdom of Juan Without Anything. Signs in the Expression of the People. Proverb.* Santa Clara, Cuba: Revista Signos. No. 14. Year 5, No. 2; January-April 1974. p. 163.

13- Álvarez de los Ríos, Tomás. *The Book of Proverbs.* Camagüey, Cuba: Editorial Ácana; 2017. p. 21.

14- Solís, José Antonio. *Proverbs, Sayings, Idioms, and Sentences. All the Popular Wisdom of the People of Spain at Your Reach.* Spain: El Arca de Papel Editores; 2003. p. 77.

15- The proverb collected by Tomás Álvarez de los Ríos is: "Absence and salty water erase love." In: Álvarez de los Ríos, Tomás. *The Book of Proverbs.* Camagüey, Cuba: Editorial Ácana; 2017. p. 68.

16- Feijóo, Samuel. *The Wisdom of Juan Without Anything. Signs in the Expression of the People. Proverb.* Santa Clara, Cuba: Revista Signos. No. 14. Year 5, No. 2; January-April 1974. p. 202.

17- Feijóo, Samuel. *The Wisdom of Juan Without Anything. Signs in the Expression of the People. Proverb.* Santa Clara,

Cuba: Revista Signos. No. 14. Year 5, No. 2; January-April 1974. p. 195.

18- Feijóo, Samuel. The Wisdom of Juan Without Anything. Signs in the Expression of the People. Proverb. Santa Clara, Cuba: Revista Signos. No. 14. Year 5, No. 2; January-April 1974. p. 54.

19- United Bible Societies. God Speaks Today. The Bible with Deuterocanonical Books. Popular Version. Second Edition. Old Testament. Ecclesiastes. Mexico City: United Bible Societies; 1987. p. 612.

20- Feijóo, Samuel. The Wisdom of Juan Without Anything. Signs in the Expression of the People. Proverb. Santa Clara, Cuba: Revista Signos. No. 14. Year 5, No. 2; January-April 1974. p. 104.

21- Solís, José Antonio. Proverbs, Sayings, Idioms, and Sentences. All the Popular Wisdom of the People of Spain at Your Reach. *La Coruña, Spain: El Arca de Papel Editores; 2003. p. 35.*

22- Flores-Huerta, Samuel. Sayings or Proverbs. Thematic Compendium. *Mexico: CopIt-arXives; 2016. p. 43.*

23- Sintes Pros, Jorge. Dictionary of Aphorisms, Proverbs, and Sayings. *Barcelona, Spain: Editorial Sintes; 1954. p. 99.*

24- Solís, José Antonio. Proverbs, Sayings, Idioms, and Sentences. All the Popular Wisdom of the People of Spain at Your Reach. *Spain: El Arca de Papel Editores; 2003. p. 116.*

25- Feijóo, Samuel. From Compliment to Colloquial Expression, Oral Folklore of Cuba. *Havana City, Cuba: Editorial Letras Cubanas; 1981. p. 49.*

26- Valdés Jane, Ernesto. Divinatory Proverbs of the Caracol and Odun of Ifá. -In Cuban Santería- Documents for the History and Culture of Osha-Ifá in Cuba. *Proverbs of Irete Ka. First Edition: Proyecto Orunmila; 2007. p. 119.*

27- *Valdés Jane, Ernesto.* Divinatory Proverbs of the Caracol and Odun of Ifá. -In Cuban Santería- Documents for the History and Culture of Osha-Ifá in Cuba. *Proverbs of (6-15) Obara tonti Marunlá. First Edition: Proyecto Orunmila; 2007. p. 24.*

28- *The proverb collected by José Antonio Solís is: "He who has shame neither dines nor lunches." In: Solís, José Antonio.* Proverbs, Sayings, Idioms, and Sentences. All the Popular Wisdom of the People of Spain at Your Reach. *Spain: El Arca de Papel Editores; 2003. p. 60.*

29- *Feijóo, Samuel.* The Wisdom of Juan Without Anything. Signs in the Expression of the People. *Proverb. Santa Clara, Cuba:* Revista Signos. *No. 14. Year 5, No. 2; January-April 1974. p. 30.*

30- *Feijóo, Samuel.* The Wisdom of Juan Without Anything. Signs in the Expression of the People. *Proverb. Santa Clara, Cuba:* Revista Signos. *No. 14. Year 5, No. 2; January-April 1974. p. 206.*

31- *Solís, José Antonio.* Proverbs, Sayings, Idioms, and Sentences. All the Popular Wisdom of the People of Spain at Your Reach. *Spain: El Arca de Papel Editores; 2003. p. 72.*

32- *Solís, José Antonio.* Proverbs, Sayings, Idioms, and Sentences. All the Popular Wisdom of the People of Spain at Your Reach. *Spain: El Arca de Papel Editores; 2003. p. 132.*

33- *Solís, José Antonio.* Proverbs, Sayings, Idioms, and Sentences. All the Popular Wisdom of the People of Spain at Your Reach. *Spain: El Arca de Papel Editores; 2003. p. 142.*

34- *Valdés Jane, Ernesto.* Divinatory Proverbs of the Caracol and Odun of Ifá. -In Cuban Santería- Documents for the History and Culture of Osha-Ifá in Cuba. *Proverbs of (3-6) Ogundá tonti Obara. First Edition: Proyecto Orunmila; 2007. p. 10.*

35- *Valdés Jane, Ernesto.* Divinatory Proverbs of the Caracol and Odun of Ifá. -In Cuban Santería- Documents for the History and Culture of Osha-Ifá in Cuba. *Proverbs of (3-13) Ogundá tonti Metanlá and Ogunda Ka. First Edition: Proyecto Orunmila; 2007. p. 12 and 102.*

36- *Solís, José Antonio.* Proverbs, Sayings, Idioms, and Sentences. All the Popular Wisdom of the People of Spain at Your Reach. *Spain: El Arca de Papel Editores; 2003. p. 67.*

37- *Solís, José Antonio.* Proverbs, Sayings, Idioms, and Sentences. All the Popular Wisdom of the People of Spain at Your Reach. *Spain: El Arca de Papel Editores; 2003. p. 126.*

38- *Feijóo, Samuel.* The Wisdom of Juan Without Anything. Signs in the Expression of the People. *Proverb. Santa Clara, Cuba:* Revista Signos. *No. 14. Year 5, No. 2; January-April 1974. p. 105.*

39- *Valdés Jane, Ernesto.* Divinatory Proverbs of the Caracol and Odun of Ifá. -In Cuban Santería- Documents for the History and Culture of Osha-Ifá in Cuba. *Proverbs of (6-9) Obara tonti Osá. First Edition: Proyecto Orunmila; 2007. p. 23.*

40- *Valdés Jane, Ernesto.* Divinatory Proverbs of the Caracol and Odun of Ifá. -In Cuban Santería- Documents for the History and Culture of Osha-Ifá in Cuba. *Proverbs of Oshe Nilogbe. First Edition: Proyecto Orunmila; 2007. p. 121.*

41- *Feijóo, Samuel. The Wisdom of Juan Without Anything. Signs in the Expression of the People. Proverb. Santa Clara, Cuba: Revista Signos. No. 14. Year 5, No. 2; January-April 1974. p. 86.*

42- *Feijóo, Samuel. The Wisdom of Juan Without Anything. Signs in the Expression of the People. Proverb. Santa Clara, Cuba: Revista Signos. No. 14. Year 5, No. 2; January-April 1974. p. 133.*

43- *The proverb collected by José Antonio Solís is: "To rage and marry poorly, it's all the same." In: Solís, José Antonio.*

Proverbs, Sayings, Idioms, and Sentences. All the Popular Wisdom. Spain: El Arca de Papel Editores; 2003. p. 137.

44- Maldonado, Felipe CR. Being and Time. Themes of Spain. Classical Spanish Proverbs and Other Popular Sayings. Madrid, Spain: Taurus Ediciones S.A.; 1960. p. 139.

45- Solís, José Antonio. Proverbs, Sayings, Idioms, and Sentences. All the Popular Wisdom. Spain: El Arca de Papel Editores; 2003. p. 42.

46- Feijóo, Samuel. The Wisdom of Juan Without Anything. Signs in the Expression of the People. Proverb. Santa Clara, Cuba: Revista Signos. No. 14. Year 5, No. 2; January-April 1974. p. 62.

47- The proverb collected by José Antonio Solís is: "Illness and old age, always hand in hand." In: Solís, José Antonio. Proverbs, Sayings, Idioms, and Sentences. All the Popular Wisdom of the People of Spain at Your Reach. Spain: El Arca de Papel Editores; 2003. p. 82.

48- The proverbs collected by Jorge Sintes Pros are: "There is no greater blind man than the one who does not want to see," and "There is no worse deaf man than the one who does not want to hear." In: Sintes Pros, Jorge. Dictionary of Aphorisms, Proverbs, and Sayings. Barcelona, Spain: Editorial Sintes; 1954. pp. 75 and 258.

49- Valdés Jane, Ernesto. Divinatory Proverbs of the Caracol and Odun of Ifá. -In Cuban Santería- Documents for the History and Culture of Osha-Ifá in Cuba. Proverbs of (10-16) Ofún tonti Merindilogún. First Edition: Proyecto Orunmila; 2007. p. 45.

50- Feijóo, Samuel. The Wisdom of Juan Without Anything. Signs in the Expression of the People. Proverb. Santa Clara, Cuba: Revista Signos. No. 14. Year 5, No. 2; January-April 1974. p. 31.

51- *Valdés Jane, Ernesto. Divinatory Proverbs of the Caracol and Odun of Ifá. -In Cuban Santería- Documents for the History and Culture of Osha-Ifá in Cuba. Proverbs of (2-4) Eyioko tonti Iroso. First Edition: Proyecto Orunmila; 2007. p. 6.*

52- *Valdés Jane, Ernesto. Divinatory Proverbs of the Caracol and Odun of Ifá. -In Cuban Santería- Documents for the History and Culture of Osha-Ifá in Cuba. Proverbs of (7-4) Odí tonti Iroso. First Edition: Proyecto Orunmila; 2007. p. 26.*

53- *Valdés Jane, Ernesto. Divinatory Proverbs of the Caracol and Odun of Ifá. -In Cuban Santería- Documents for the History and Culture of Osha-Ifá in Cuba. Proverbs of (4-4) Iroso tonti Iroso. First Edition: Proyecto Orunmila; 2007. p. 14.*

54- *Valdés Jane, Ernesto. Divinatory Proverbs of the Caracol and Odun of Ifá. -In Cuban Santería- Documents for the History and Culture of Osha-Ifá in Cuba. Proverbs of (2-4) Eyioko tonti Iroso. First Edition: Proyecto Orunmila; 2007. p. 5.*

55- *Feijóo, Samuel. The Wisdom of Juan Without Anything. Signs in the Expression of the People. Proverb. Santa Clara, Cuba: Revista Signos. No. 14. Year 5, No. 2; January-April 1974. p. 195.*

56- *Sarma, Vishnu. Panchatantra. Third Edition. Havana City, Cuba: Editorial Arte y Literatura; 2014. p. 178.*

57- *Feijóo, Samuel. The Wisdom of Juan Without Anything. Signs in the Expression of the People. Proverb. Santa Clara, Cuba: Revista Signos. No. 14. Year 5, No. 2; January-April 1974. p. 158.*

58- *Feijóo, Samuel. The Wisdom of Juan Without Anything. Signs in the Expression of the People. Proverb. Santa Clara, Cuba: Revista Signos. No. 14. Year 5, No. 2; January-April 1974. p. 15.*

59- Feijóo, Samuel. *The Wisdom of Juan Without Anything. Signs in the Expression of the People. Proverb. Santa Clara, Cuba: Revista Signos. No. 14. Year 5, No. 2; January-April 1974. p. 24.*

60- Feijóo, Samuel. *The Wisdom of Juan Without Anything. Signs in the Expression of the People. Proverb. Santa Clara, Cuba: Revista Signos. No. 14. Year 5, No. 2; January-April 1974. p. 179.*

61- Feijóo, Samuel. The Wisdom of Juan Without Anything. Signs in the Expression of the People. *Proverb. Santa Clara, Cuba:* Revista Signos. *No. 14. Year 5, No. 2; January-April 1974. p. 133.*

62- Feijóo, Samuel. The Wisdom of Juan Without Anything. Signs in the Expression of the People. *Proverb. Santa Clara, Cuba:* Revista Signos. *No. 14. Year 5, No. 2; January-April 1974. p. 146.*

63- *Carnegie, Dale.* How to Win Friends and Influence People. *Rosario, Argentina: Biblioteca del Nuevo Tiempo. 104th edition: September 1996. p. 10. Adhered to: Directorio Promineo:* www.promineo.gq.nu.

64- Feijóo, Samuel. The Wisdom of Juan Without Anything. Signs in the Expression of the People. *Proverb. Santa Clara, Cuba:* Revista Signos. *No. 14. Year 5, No. 2; January-April 1974. p. 195.*

65- *Solís, José Antonio.* Proverbs, Sayings, Idioms, and Sentences. All the Popular Wisdom of the People of Spain at Your Reach. *Spain: El Arca de Papel Editores; 2003. p. 126.*

66- *Feijóo, Samuel.* From Compliment to Colloquial Expression, Oral Folklore of Cuba. *Havana City, Cuba: Editorial Letras Cubanas; 1981. p. 30.*

67- Feijóo, Samuel. The Wisdom of Juan Without Anything. Signs in the Expression of the People. *Proverb. Santa Clara, Cuba:* Revista Signos. *No. 14. Year 5, No. 2; January-April 1974. p. 206.*

68- *Valdés Jane, Ernesto.* Divinatory Proverbs of the Caracol and Odun of Ifá. -In Cuban Santería- Documents for the History and Culture of Osha-Ifá in Cuba. *Proverbs of Otura Bara. First Edition: Proyecto Orunmila; 2007. p. 115.*

69- *The proverb collected by Samuel Flores Huerta is: "Loneliness is a very bad counselor." In: Flores-Huerta, Samuel.* Sayings or Proverbs. Thematic Compendium. *Mexico: CopIt-arXives; 2016. p. 136.*

70- *Confucius in: Lin Yutang.* The Wisdom of Confucius. *Buenos Aires, Argentina: Ediciones Siglo Veinte; 1952. p. 174.*

71- *Sintes Pros, Jorge.* Dictionary of Aphorisms, Proverbs, and Sayings. *Barcelona, Spain: Editorial Sintes; 1954. p. 268.*

72- *United Bible Societies.* God Speaks Today. The Bible with Deuterocanonical Books. Deuterocanonical Books. Ecclesiasticus. *Popular Version. Second Edition. Mexico City: United Bible Societies; 1987. p. 96.*

73- *Martí, José.* Complete Works. *Vol. II. Commemorative Edition of the Fiftieth Anniversary of His Death. Havana: Editorial Lex; 1946. p. 1892.*

74- *Feijóo, Samuel.* The Wisdom of Juan Without Anything. Signs in the Expression of the People. *Proverb. Santa Clara, Cuba:* Revista Signos. *No. 14. Year 5, No. 2; January-April 1974. p. 139.*

75- *Valdés Jane, Ernesto.* Divinatory Proverbs of the Caracol and Odun of Ifá. -In Cuban Santería- Documents for the History and Culture of Osha-Ifá in Cuba. *Proverbs of (9-13) Osá tonti Metanlá and Osa Ka. First Edition: Proyecto Orunmila; 2007. pp. 39 and 106.*

76- *United Bible Societies.* God Speaks Today. The Bible with Deuterocanonical Books. New Testament. Saint Matthew. *Popular Version. Second Edition. Mexico City: United Bible Societies; 1987. p. 7.*

77- *Feijóo, Samuel.* The Wisdom of Juan Without Anything. Signs in the Expression of the People. *Proverb. Santa Clara, Cuba:* Revista Signos. *No. 14. Year 5, No. 2; January-April 1974. p. 58.*

78- *Valdés Jane, Ernesto.* Divinatory Proverbs of the Caracol and Odun of Ifá. -In Cuban Santería- Documents for the History and Culture of Osha-Ifá in Cuba. *Proverbs of (14-3) Merinlá tonti Ogundá. First Edition: Proyecto Orunmila; 2007. p. 57.*

79- *Feijóo, Samuel.* The Wisdom of Juan Without Anything. Signs in the Expression of the People. *Proverb. Santa Clara, Cuba:* Revista Signos. *No. 14. Year 5, No. 2; January-April 1974. p. 63.*

80- *Valdés Jane, Ernesto.* Divinatory Proverbs of the Caracol and Odun of Ifá. -In Cuban Santería- Documents for the History and Culture of Osha-Ifá in Cuba. *Proverbs of (7-4) Odí tonti Iroso. First Edition: Proyecto Orunmila; 2007. p. 26.*

81- *Rovira, Àlex. Words that Heal. Barcelona, Spain: Plataforma Editorial; 2008. p. 25.*

82- *The proverb collected by Samuel Feijóo is: "Everyone plays their own hand." In: Feijóo, Samuel. From Compliment to Colloquial Expression, Oral Folklore of Cuba. Havana City, Cuba: Editorial Letras Cubanas; 1981. p. 32.*

83- *Feijóo, Samuel. The Wisdom of Juan Without Anything. Signs in the Expression of the People. Proverb. Santa Clara, Cuba: Revista Signos. No. 14. Year 5, No. 2; January-April 1974. p. 99.*

84- *Feijóo, Samuel. From Compliment to Colloquial Expression, Oral Folklore of Cuba. Havana City, Cuba: Editorial Letras Cubanas; 1981. p. 24.*

85- *Sintes Pros, Jorge. Dictionary of Aphorisms, Proverbs, and Sayings. Barcelona, Spain: Editorial Sintes; 1954. p. 216.*

86- *Sintes Pros, Jorge. Dictionary of Aphorisms, Proverbs, and Sayings. Barcelona, Spain: Editorial Sintes; 1954. p. 99.*

87- *Feijóo, Samuel. The Wisdom of Juan Without Anything. Signs in the Expression of the People. Proverb. Santa Clara, Cuba: Revista Signos. No. 14. Year 5, No. 2; January-April 1974. p. 178.*

88- *Feijóo, Samuel. From Compliment to Colloquial Expression, Oral Folklore of Cuba. Havana City, Cuba: Editorial Letras Cubanas; 1981. p. 37.*

89- *Feijóo, Samuel. From Compliment to Colloquial Expression, Oral Folklore of Cuba. Havana City, Cuba: Editorial Letras Cubanas; 1981. p. 26.*

90- *Feijóo, Samuel. The Wisdom of Juan Without Anything. Signs in the Expression of the People. Proverb. Santa Clara, Cuba: Revista Signos. No. 14. Year 5, No. 2; January-April 1974. p. 178.*

91- *United Bible Societies. God Speaks Today. The Bible with Deuterocanonical Books. Old Testament. Proverbs. Popular Version. Second Edition. Mexico City: United Bible Societies; 1987. p. 598.*

92- *Valdés Jane, Ernesto. Divinatory Proverbs of the Caracol and Odun of Ifá. -In Cuban Santería- Documents for the History and Culture of Osha-Ifá in Cuba. Proverbs of (14-2) Merinlá Tonti Eyioko. First Edition: Proyecto Orunmila; 2007. p. 57.*

93- *Valdés Jane, Ernesto. Divinatory Proverbs of the Caracol and Odun of Ifá. -In Cuban Santería- Documents for the History and Culture of Osha-Ifá in Cuba. Proverbs of Oshe Bile. First Edition: Proyecto Orunmila; 2007. p. 123.*

94- The proverb collected by Ernesto Valdés Jane is: "War is won with a good strategy, but by force, it is lost." In: Valdés Jane, Ernesto. Divinatory Proverbs of the Caracol and Odun of Ifá. -In Cuban Santería- Documents for the History and Culture of Osha-Ifá in Cuba. Proverbs of (8-12) Eyeúnle tonti Eyilá. First Edition: Proyecto Orunmila; 2007. p. 33.

95- Solís, José Antonio. Proverbs, Sayings, Idioms, and Sentences. All the Popular Wisdom of the People of Spain at Your Reach. Spain: El Arca de Papel Editores; 2003. p. 150.

96- Feijóo, Samuel. The Wisdom of Juan Without Anything. Signs in the Expression of the People. Proverb. Santa Clara, Cuba: Revista Signos. No. 14. Year 5, No. 2; January-April 1974. p. 161.

97- Feijóo, Samuel. The Wisdom of Juan Without Anything. Signs in the Expression of the People. Proverb. Santa Clara, Cuba: Revista Signos. No. 14. Year 5, No. 2; January-April 1974. p. 200.

98- Solís, José Antonio. Proverbs, Sayings, Idioms, and Sentences. All the Popular Wisdom of the People of Spain at Your Reach. Spain: El Arca de Papel Editores; 2003. p. 123.

99- Feijóo, Samuel. The Wisdom of Juan Without Anything. Signs in the Expression of the People. Proverb. Santa Clara, Cuba: Revista Signos. No. 14. Year 5, No. 2; January-April 1974. p. 163.

100- Feijóo, Samuel. The Wisdom of Juan Without Anything. Signs in the Expression of the People. Proverb. Santa Clara, Cuba: Revista Signos. No. 14. Year 5, No. 2; January-April 1974. p. 67.

101- Martí, José. General Correspondence. To His Sister Amelia. In: Complete Works, Vol. XX. Havana, Cuba: Editorial de Ciencias Sociales; 1991. p. 287.

102- Feijóo, Samuel. The Wisdom of Juan Without Anything. Signs in the Expression of the People. Proverb. Santa Clara,

Cuba: Revista Signos. No. 14. Year 5, No. 2; January-April 1974. p. 204.

103- Feijóo, Samuel. The Wisdom of Juan Without Anything. Signs in the Expression of the People. Proverb. Santa Clara, Cuba: Revista Signos. No. 14. Year 5, No. 2; January-April 1974. p. 26.

104- Feijóo, Samuel. The Wisdom of Juan Without Anything. Signs in the Expression of the People. Proverb. Santa Clara, Cuba: Revista Signos. No. 14. Year 5, No. 2; January-April 1974. p. 156.

105- The proverb collected by Tomás Álvarez de los Ríos is: "He who has a shop, let him attend it; otherwise, let him sell it." In: Álvarez de los Ríos, Tomás. The Book of Proverbs. Camagüey, Cuba: Editorial Ácana; 2017. p. 53.

106- Feijóo, Samuel. The Wisdom of Juan Without Anything. Signs in the Expression of the People. Proverb. Santa Clara, Cuba: Revista Signos. No. 14. Year 5, No. 2; January-April 1974. p. 130.

107- Solís, José Antonio. Proverbs, Sayings, Idioms, and Sentences. All the Popular Wisdom of the People of Spain at Your Reach. Spain: El Arca de Papel Editores; 2003. p. 120.

108- Solís, José Antonio. Proverbs, Sayings, Idioms, and Sentences. All the Popular Wisdom of the People of Spain at Your Reach. Spain: El Arca de Papel Editores; 2003. p. 120.

109- Lao Tse. Tao Teh Ching. In: Lin Yutang. Chinese Wisdom. Buenos Aires, Argentina: Colección ACADEMUS, Biblioteca Nueva; 1945. p. 59.

110- Lao Tse. Tao Teh Ching. In: Lin Yutang. Chinese Wisdom. Buenos Aires, Argentina: Colección ACADEMUS, Biblioteca Nueva; 1945. p. 58.

111- Feijóo, Samuel. The Wisdom of Juan Without Anything. Signs in the Expression of the People. Proverb. Santa Clara,

Cuba: Revista Signos. No. 14. Year 5, No. 2; January-April 1974. p. 159.

112- Valdés Jane, Ernesto. Divinatory Proverbs of the Caracol and Odun of Ifá. -In Cuban Santería- Documents for the History and Culture of Osha-Ifá in Cuba. Proverbs of (1-1) Okana tonti Okana and Okana Meyi. First Edition: Proyecto Orunmila; 2007. pp. 1 and 95.

113- Feijóo, Samuel. The Wisdom of Juan Without Anything. Signs in the Expression of the People. Proverb. Santa Clara, Cuba: Revista Signos. No. 14. Year 5, No. 2; January-April 1974. p. 87.

114- Valdés Jane, Ernesto. Divinatory Proverbs of the Caracol and Odun of Ifá. -In Cuban Santería- Documents for the History and Culture of Osha-Ifá in Cuba. Proverbs of (13-7) Metanlá tonti Odí. First Edition: Proyecto Orunmila; 2007. p. 55.

115- Feijóo, Samuel. The Wisdom of Juan Without Anything. Signs in the Expression of the People. Proverb. Santa Clara, Cuba: Revista Signos. No. 14. Year 5, No. 2; January-April 1974. p. 52.

116- Feijóo, Samuel. The Wisdom of Juan Without Anything. Signs in the Expression of the People. Proverb. Santa Clara, Cuba: Revista Signos. No. 14. Year 5, No. 2; January-April 1974. p. 178.

117- Valdés Jane, Ernesto. Divinatory Proverbs of the Caracol and Odun of Ifá. -In Cuban Santería- Documents for the History and Culture of Osha-Ifá in Cuba. Proverbs of (1-1) Okana tonti Okana. First Edition: Proyecto Orunmila; 2007. p. 1.

118- Solís, José Antonio. Proverbs, Sayings, Idioms, and Sentences. All the Popular Wisdom of the People of Spain at Your Reach. Spain: El Arca de Papel Editores; 2003. p. 89.

119- Solís, José Antonio. Proverbs, Sayings, Idioms, and Sentences. All the Popular Wisdom of the People of Spain at Your Reach. Spain: El Arca de Papel Editores; 2003. p. 109.

120- Confucius in: Lin Yutang. The Wisdom of Confucius. Buenos Aires, Argentina: Ediciones Siglo Veinte; 1952. p. 174.

121- Feijóo, Samuel. The Wisdom of Juan Without Anything. Signs in the Expression of the People. *Proverb. Santa Clara, Cuba:* Revista Signos. *No. 14. Year 5, No. 2; January-April 1974. p. 130.*

122- Feijóo, Samuel. From Compliment to Colloquial Expression, Oral Folklore of Cuba. *Havana City, Cuba: Editorial Letras Cubanas; 1981. p. 24.*

123- Feijóo, Samuel. The Wisdom of Juan Without Anything. Signs in the Expression of the People. *Proverb. Santa Clara, Cuba:* Revista Signos. *No. 14. Year 5, No. 2; January-April 1974. p. 99.*

124- Martí, José. Our America. The Prehistoric Chronology of America. *In:* Complete Works, *Vol. VIII. Havana, Cuba: Editorial de Ciencias Sociales; 1991. p. 341.*

125- Feijóo, Samuel. The Wisdom of Juan Without Anything. Signs in the Expression of the People. *Proverb. Santa Clara, Cuba:* Revista Signos. *No. 14. Year 5, No. 2; January-April 1974. p. 67.*

126- The proverb collected by Tomás Álvarez de los Ríos is: "He who has a shop, let him attend it; otherwise, let him sell it." In: Álvarez de los Ríos, Tomás. The Book of Proverbs. *Camagüey, Cuba: Editorial Ácana; 2017. p. 53.*

127- Clavijo Portieles, Alberto. Crisis, Family, and Psychotherapy. *Second Edition. Havana, Cuba: Editorial Ciencias Médicas; 2011. p. 6.*

128- *Clavijo Portieles, Alberto.* Crisis, Family, and Psychotherapy. *Second Edition. Havana, Cuba: Editorial Ciencias Médicas;* 2011. p. 6.

~~~